Joy in Learning
A Gift of Poems to the Young

Ebenezer Sowa Klufio

Illustrations by: Joseph Ingking

Order this book online at www.trafford.com
or email orders@trafford.com

Most Trafford titles are also available at major online book retailers.

 www.trafford.com

North America & international
toll-free: 844 688 6899 (USA & Canada)
fax: 812 355 4082

Our mission is to efficiently provide the world's finest, most comprehensive book publishing service, enabling every author to experience success. To find out how to publish your book, your way, and have it available worldwide, visit us online at www.trafford.com

Because of the dynamic nature of the Internet, any web addresses or links contained in this book may have changed since publication and may no longer be valid. The views expressed in this work are solely those of the author and do not necessarily reflect the views of the publisher, and the publisher hereby disclaims any responsibility for them.

Illustrations by: Joseph Ingking

ISBN: 978-1-4669-7337-4 (sc)
978-1-4669-7338-1 (e)

Library of Congress Control Number: 2012923869

Print information available on the last page.

Trafford rev. 03/02/2021

This work is dedicated to my darling wife Edwina, the light of my life and my inspiration.

FOREWORD

This collection provides a lively spread of poems that cover just about any aspect of a child's growing up and life experiences. The surreal scenarios played out in some of the poems such as "The Friend in the Mirror" depict very real life experiences.

These poems were written just for sheer fun; some will make you smile and reminisce, some you may not entirely understand, some are for pleasure in sounds and rhymes, and others have been written to arouse a child's curiosity and amuse. Poetry is certainly a way of capturing the essence of life. It is a way of sharing experiences and feelings, and in the end, it does a good job of entertaining us all.

This is for both children and adults to enjoy, so whichever you are, indulge yourself in the richness of the collection. Learn something from it, for in the end, there is joy in learning.

E. S. Klufio, 2012

The Busy Lorry Park

They come through one entrance.
They go out by the same exit.
But in between the two,
They toot, honk, back, and brake,
While shoppers and hawkers, some
With wares on their heads or babies
On their backs, dash to one side
Or start, swerve, and stumble
In a busy lorry park.

But some cars, once stopped,
Will not start again,
For batteries are weak
And replacements rare,
But never is this a problem.
The long snaking queues
Do quite readily provide

More hands than needed.
Push! The engine kicks off!

There is, at once, a scramble
For places in the car,
As if pushing should
For each a seat ensure,
But some do push and lose.
For sure, does it turn out,
The car goes not their way,
And they rejoin queues
In the busy lorry park!

Eating at the Table

About eating at the table,
There is much to learn.
Though this calls for effort,
It's rather not too trying.

Words like plate and flat,
Bowl and deep,
Pot and dish,
Cup and glass,
Words like fried and grilled,
Boiled and baked
All a part do play.

So knife is right,
And fork is left,
And spoon by knife must lie.
With rice and stew comes
Fork and knife.
But if it's fufu,

Then soup comes in company,
And thus the choice
Of using your fingers
Or a spoon and fork.

Whichever it is you use,
Ensure they are clean,
As "cleanliness is Godliness."

Sweets Are Sweet

Baby's cry of hunger
Rings shrilly through the house.
Mama hurries to pick up baby.

She takes out her tender breast
And offers, with loving care,
Nature's most nutritious milk.

Though unmatched in quality,
This cannot in any way
Be described as sweet to taste.

But it does not take long
For Mama to firmly decide,
Baby needs more than what
Two full breasts can give.

So some porridge is prepared,
But being of different taste
From the more familiar milk,
Sugar is added
With very good results,
For baby needs no coaxing
To suck full bottles dry.

And so with Mama's help
Does it come about
Indeed quite naturally,
That from food not too sweet,
Baby soon learns to prefer
What is sweet, sweet, and sweet.

Darling baby eats and grows
And, in growing, becomes a child,
Who learns that Mama's approach
Is not at all peculiar.

For medicines come as syrup,
Which is mercifully sweet,
And the doctor uses toffee
To get the needed co-operation.

There is also Daddy,
Who must bring home chocolate
To leave for work in peace.
Oh! Sweets are indeed sweet
But demand care for the teeth.

Then the dearest aunt
Who visits quite regularly
And never fails to produce
From bag, purse, or pocket
Candy, candy after candy,
So true is she to this habit,
Her appearance always makes
Mouths water and water
Each preparing to receive
Its more-than-certain share
Of what has just arrived.
Ah! Sweets are surely sweet
But demand care for the teeth.

Now what there is in sweets
That so pleases children
The same, once in the mouth,
Grow lots of germs that cause
Gum pains and toothache,
Unless properly dealt with
By good oral hygiene.
But God in his wisdom,
Knowing children's weakness,
Has given yet another chance
In a second set of teeth.
Oh! Ah! Sweets are sweet
But demand care for the teeth.

Going to Bed

Every night at eight-thirty,
Mama orders, "Off to bed!"
"Why this early?" we complain.
"Just like food," Daddy says,
"Sleep is good for growing up."
A grown-up's growing is done.
A child's growing has just begun,
So to bed early children must go
To grow up as well as they should.

I Know a Trick or Two

I know Mama is worried.
Though she has lots to do,
She must collect my dress
From the maker's by six.
If she would only ask,
I could make it, walk over,
And get home right on time.
Oh! I know a trick or two.

Were it even to rain,
I could make it, dash off,
Take the nearest minibus,
And reach home dry and clean
To Mama's joy and delight.
I know a trick or two.
Just wait and you'll see.

The dress I shall wear
With pride and smiles
For our visit to Grandpa's.
Over there where they live
Is a tall guava tree,
Which keeps its fruits high
And out of reach for us all.

But Grandpa must insist
We take home some fruits
And has a fruit plucker ready
To bring down fruit after fruit
And watches us dash about
As, with bounce and glee,
We pick them one by one.

No one thinks of asking,
But I could, with ease, make
Branch on branch bend down
To offer fruits for plucking.
Oh! I know a trick or two.
I am waiting and waiting,
Yes, waiting yet to show
I know a trick or two.

Warm and Cozy

Early in the morning,
When sheets are warm
And sleep is cozy,
Daddy comes to wake us.
He shakes and tugs.
He pushes and pulls.
"Yes," we say to him,
"We shall get up at once,"

As from bed we rise.
He then goes off to do
Some of the morning's chores.
But sheets still are warm
And sleep still cozy.

Soon, and much too soon,
Back, alas, he comes
With shouts and threats
To wake us up this time
With a sprinkling
Of ice-cold water.

We do get up as we should,
But not for the threats.
We've heard them twice,
Thrice, and more before.

The Friend in the Mirror

Every day after bath
As I walk to the mirror,
A friend comes to meet me.
She looks so much like me.
I call her Mirror-me.
I greet her with a smile,
Which she warmly returns.
As with my right I powder,
She does it with her left.

I tell her, "Use your right!"
She appears not to hear.
So as my left I stretch
To pick up my comb or brush,
She reaches out for hers
Nimbly with her right.
It is only in this way
She is different from me.

What on my face I have
With only fingers felt,
Her face does allow me
Very clearly to see.
Pleased with myself,
I smile and say good-bye,
And as I turn to go,
She also does the same.

Should I but look back,
She turns to attend to me
And only leaves me finally
When I look back no more.

Of Life and Cycle Changes

The sun rises and sets
To give us day and night.
The rains come down, then stop
According to year's seasons.
The clock ticks ticktock
So we can tell the hour.
Most cyclic changes
Are basic to life.

Wings flap up and down,
Keeping birds in flight.
Oars rise then hurtle down
As boats glide on water.
Feet plunge down and rise
As bicycles take us home.
Most cyclic changes
Are basic to life.

Balls bounce up and down,
Inviting kick or touch.
Swings swing to and fro
For the pleasure of children.
Hands clap, clap, and clap,
Expressing cheer and joy.
Most cyclic changes
Are basic to life.

The school bell rings
And rings to send us home.
Hands wave to and fro
As we bid good-bye.
Flags flutter in salute
To the living or the dead.
Most cyclic changes
Are basic to life.

'tick tock tick tock tick tock'

Printed in the United States
By Bookmasters